Anne Fran Legacy

Jemma J. Saunders

Copyright © Jemma J. Saunders 2015

The right of Jemma J. Saunders to be identified as the author of this work has been asserted by her in accordance with the Copyright, Designs and Patents Act, 1988.

First published in 2015 by Endeavour Press Ltd.

Table of Contents

Introduction	5
Part One: Frankfurt and Amsterdam	7
A German Family	9
The Nazi Shadow	13
Refuge in Amsterdam	16
Life under Occupation	20
Receiving the Diary	25
Part Two: A Clandestine Existence	28
The Secret Annexe	29
Eight Jews in Hiding	32
Daily Life in the Annexe	36
The Helpers	41
Constant Fear: Bombs and Burglaries	45
An Isolated Adolescence	48
Rewriting the Diary	52
Part Three: The Final Solution	55

The Arrest: 4 August 1944	56
Westerbork and Deportation	59
Two Months in Auschwitz	62
Alone in Bergen-Belsen	66
Otto's Return	69
The Diary Saved	72
Part Four: Posthumous Fame	75
Publishing Het Achterhuis	76
Broadway and Hollywood	79
The Anne Frank House	83
Authenticating the Diary	86
Who Betrayed Anne Frank?	89
Anne's Legacy	92
Select Bibliography	94

Introduction

Anne Frank is arguably the most well-known victim of the Holocaust, the 20th century genocide in which some six million Jews were systematically murdered in Europe under the Nazi regime. Born into a well-to-do, liberal Jewish family in Germany at the end of the 1920s, almost the entire course of her life was determined by the rise of the Nazi party: from the day her family fled Germany to build a new life in Amsterdam in 1933; to the twenty-five months they spent hiding in the back of a warehouse before the tragedy of their betrayal and deportation. Anne was just 15 years old when she perished in Bergen-Belsen concentration camp in 1945.

The teenage Anne started keeping a diary shortly before the Frank family went into hiding in 1942, and over the course of two years she honed her craft as a writer, documenting the details of their daily lives alongside her personal reflections, fears, and aspirations. By chance, the majority of her writings were saved after the family was arrested and in 1947, after much deliberation, her father oversaw the publication of the first edition of her diary in the Netherlands. Within a decade, it had become an international bestseller. First adapted for both stage and screen in the 1950s, awareness and readership of Anne's diary continued to grow and its author became a household name, gradually acquiring something of a symbolic status.

In the intervening years, the diary has had its share of critics as well as champions, and to this day there are those who refute that the historical events that surround its writing and publication ever took place. Nevertheless, in the 21st Century, *The Diary of a Young Girl* remains one of the most widely read non-fiction books in the world and Anne Frank's story, whether portrayed in writing, film or on the stage, continues to evoke curiosity and emotion.

Part One: Frankfurt and Amsterdam

A German Family

Annelies Marie Frank was born on 12 June 1929 in the German city of Frankfurt-am-Main. She was the second daughter of Otto Frank and Edith Holländer, who had married in Aachen on 12 May 1925. An older sister, Margot Betti, had been born on 16 February 1926.

Otto Frank celebrated his 36th birthday the day he married Edith Holländer, who was almost eleven years his junior. It is not clear how the couple met, but it is probable that the marriage was a matter of practicality as well as love, since Edith had a considerable dowry. Both came from assimilated German Jewish families, although Edith maintained a stronger connection to Judaism than her husband, who seldom attended synagogue, had not had a Bar Mitzvah and had never learned Hebrew. Edith, on the other hand, had grown up in a kosher household in the northern city of Aachen and continued to attend synagogue when she moved with Otto to Frankfurt, where his family owned a small but prosperous bank.

Both Otto and Edith could trace their families' roots in Germany back generations; in Otto's case beyond the 1700s. He was the second of four children, three brothers and a sister born in the last decades of the 19th century. Edith had two surviving older brothers, Julius and Walter, and was from a reasonably wealthy industrial family, prominent among Aachen's Jewish community. Her sister Bettina had died of appendicitis when Edith was just 14, and twelve years later Edith later chose Margot's middle name, Betti, in memory of her.

As a young man Otto studied economics for a year at Heidelberg University, but he decided not to continue his studies and instead travelled to New York, where he worked in Macy's department store. His American adventure was cut short, however, by the unexpected death of his father Michael in September 1909, though he did later return to the USA and maintained a lifelong friendship with the son of Macy's owner. When World War One broke out, Otto became one of 100,000 Jews to serve in the Germany Army during the conflict, rising to the rank of lieutenant. His future brother-in-law Julius Holländer also fought in the war and both families considered themselves German first and foremost. In the years following the armistice, Otto took more responsibility in the family business, attempting to open a branch of the bank in Amsterdam in 1923. This venture proved unsuccessful and he returned to Frankfurt, though his connection with Amsterdam would prove important a decade later.

After his marriage to Edith and their honeymoon in Italy, Otto returned to work in the bank. The newlywed couple boarded with his mother, Alice Frank, in the large family home on Mertonstrasse until 1927, when they moved with baby Margot to an apartment of their own on Marbachweg. This was where their second daughter Annelies was brought home, twelve days after her hospital birth.

Anne, as she later became known, was something of a difficult child. Unlike her sister Margot, who had been a peaceful baby and a similarly demure toddler, Anne's infancy was characterised by sleepless nights and bouts of colic. Margot was nevertheless delighted to have a new sibling and often took Anne out for walks in her pram. Edith was a devoted mother and enjoyed domestic help in the family home from a young woman named Kathi Stilgenbauer. Perhaps unusually for a father of the era, Otto was just as involved in his daughters' upbringings as Edith. They affectionately called him 'Pim' and from an early age he incorporated education into their childhood, creating stories about two characters called 'Good Paula' and 'Bad Paula' as a means of teaching Margot and Anne about right and wrong.

The wider family circle remained in close contact and both Anne and Margot enjoyed the affections of their other relatives. Both their widowed grandmothers visited the Franks often, especially when they no longer lived with Otto's mother. While Alice was called Omi by her grandchildren, Edith's mother, Rosa Holländer, was referred to as Oma. Inquisitive and outspoken from an early age, as a toddler Anne once loudly asked commuters on a tram if any of them would offer a seat to her elderly grandmother.

The children also enjoyed visits from Edith's brothers, Julius and Walter, who had no children of their own but adored their nieces. Among Otto's siblings, only his sister Leni and her husband Erich Elias had children; two boys called Stephan and Bernhard, who was usually known as Buddy but whom Anne called Bernd. Stephan was born in 1921 and Buddy in 1925. Although closest in age to Margot, Buddy would later reflect more on his connection to Anne, with whom he shared a mischievous kinship.

The Franks, Holländers and Eliases marked Jewish festivals throughout the year and although Anne and Margot were not brought up in an orthodox Jewish home, they were by no means unaware of their family's religious heritage. At the time of Anne's birth, all her immediate family lived in Germany. Within a decade, economic and political circumstance would see them scattered across five countries and two continents.

The Nazi Shadow

Around four months after Anne was born, in October 1929, the Wall Street stock market crashed in America, prompting the worldwide depression of the 1930s. For a family like the Franks, whose livelihood centred on banking, the Wall Street Crash was no small impediment to their wellbeing. Indeed, the impact across Germany as a whole was keenly felt. Businesses were once again in the midst of financial crisis, having barely recovered from the economic turmoil that had followed the end of World War One. Erich Elias, recognising a more promising opportunity, moved to Switzerland in late 1929 and began making arrangements for Leni and his boys to join him over the next couple of years.

The Franks moved from Marbachweg to a smaller apartment in March 1931, when Anne was nearly two. Whether this was entirely due to financial difficulties is unclear, as their landlord at Marbachweg was a staunch Nazi party supporter and may have given the family notice because they were Jewish. Otto and Edith were fully aware of Adolf Hitler's anti-Semitic ideology and the repercussions it could have for German Jews if his *Nationalsozialistische Deutsche Arbeiterpartei* (Nazi Party) continued to gain influence. This right-wing political party had been formed in 1920 and Hitler, a demagogic Austrian, had become its leader in 1921.

In his 1925 book, *Mein Kampf* (*My Struggle*), Hitler had outlined his hatred for the Jewish race, declaring them a scapegoat for all Germany's social and financial difficulties. For some, like the Franks, this text was an early warning of the party's stance towards Jews. Indeed, following Hitler's election as Chancellor in January 1933, the situation in Germany intensified. As the Nazi shadow fell across the country in the early 1930s, it became increasingly difficult for Jews to maintain their assimilated status in society. The already severe economic effects of the Wall Street Crash, which had significantly impacted on the Frank family's stability, were exacerbated by the Nazi rise to power, as anti-Semitic decrees were introduced that made it ever harder for Jewish businesses to operate. Anti-Semitism was by no means an unknown force in Germany, but under the Nazis it developed an increasingly threatening momentum.

On 1 April 1933, shortly after Hitler attained power, all Jewish businesses in Germany were subjected to a boycott, with derogatory slogans daubed on windows and Nazi soldiers positioned outside shop doors. A subsequent flurry of persecutory laws further segregated the Jewish community socially, as well as in business matters. Margot Frank, already a promising student at the age of seven, was forced to sit apart from her gentile classmates in school. Otto, who considered himself German through and through, decided that his family could not remain in the Fatherland: his daughters should not face a childhood where they were forcibly separated from their peers. There were surely, as his brother-in-law Erich had found, good business prospects elsewhere. The Franks left their apartment and moved back in with

Omi on Mertonstrasse as a temporary measure, until arrangements could be made to emigrate.

Refuge in Amsterdam

Otto Frank had developed business connections in the Netherlands during the 1920s and had a good command of the Dutch language. When an opportunity to work in Amsterdam was proposed by Erich Elias, it therefore seemed a pragmatic choice and preparations began for the family to leave Germany.

While Otto was establishing his business in Amsterdam and seeking a new family home, Edith and the children lodged with Oma in Aachen, the north German city close to the Dutch border where Edith had grown up. An apartment was eventually found at 37 Merwedeplein, a modern development in Amsterdam's River Quarter, where Edith and Margot joined Otto in late 1933. Anne did not arrive in the Netherlands until February 1934, when she was put on the table as a birthday surprise for her sister. The Merwedeplein apartment was a comfortable family home, with additional space for a tenant, located in a part of the city that became very popular among German-Jewish refugees.

Anne commenced Kindergarten at the progressive Montessori School shortly before her fifth birthday. Here she became friends with Hannah Goslar, who also lived on Merwedeplein. Like the Franks, the Goslars were Jewish and had left Germany due to the prejudices of the Nazi regime. Following the 1935 Nuremberg Laws, which defined who was Jewish under Nazi law and deprived them of their German citizenship, a further wave of Jews left their homeland. Many took refuge in the Netherlands, while others put their faith in France, Belgium, or Britain. Some even fled as far as the USA or South America in the hope of a life that was free from persecution. A multitude of decrees besides the Nuremberg Laws had been implemented to increasingly restrict the rights of Jews in Germany, segregating them from the rest of society.

Unaware of these anti-Semitic developments in the country of their birth, Anne and Hanneli, as she was called, quickly adapted to Dutch life and often played together outside school. A favourite weekend game was calling each other on the telephones in Otto's office, pretending to be secretaries. They also helped each other with homework as they progressed through their education, although neither was fond of mathematics. A third Jewish girl, Sanne Ledermann, completed a close friendship trio. Although she did not regularly attend synagogue nor learn Hebrew, unlike her sister Margot, Anne often joined Hanneli's family in celebrating Jewish religious festivals such as Passover. She continued to be a precocious child throughout the 1930s, with Hanneli's mother remarking, 'God knows everything, but Anne knows everything better'.

Margot attended a different school to Anne, the Jeker School, and excelled at her studies, remaining a model older sister who regularly brought home straight A-grade report cards. Anne, by contrast, exhibited an enquiring nature from an early age and was well-suited to the freedom offered by the Montessori schooling system. A frail child, she often missed lessons due to illness, as did

Margot, but was nevertheless popular among her peers and socialized widely outside of school. Both sisters soon spoke Dutch as fluently as their German mother tongue; indeed, as the 1930s progressed their letters to family members were increasingly written in Dutch, with Otto providing a German translation. Edith, however, struggled with the unfamiliar language and never attained the same proficiency as her daughters and husband. She remained an efficient housewife with a modest disposition, who often worried about Margot and Anne's fragile health.

The Franks steadily established friendships with other German Jewish families, including the Goslars, and hosted coffee afternoons where they could discuss the situation in Germany and reminisce about times past. Edith, especially, was homesick for her more affluent life in Frankfurt. Their social circle also included Christian acquaintances such as Otto's employee Miep Santrouschitz and her boyfriend, Jan Gies.

No members of Otto's close family remained in Germany by the end of the 1930s: his two brothers had emigrated to Paris and London, while his mother, Alice, had left Frankfurt in late 1933 to be with Leni, Erich and her grandsons in Switzerland. Although they no longer lived close by, Anne often visited her cousins Stephan and Buddy during the 1930s and a regular correspondence flourished between three generations of the family across the continent.

Although they believed themselves safe in Amsterdam, the increasingly anti-Semitic climate in Germany greatly concerned the Franks. In November 1938, Edith's brother Walter was one of 248 Jewish men from Aachen arrested during the Nazi's *Kristallnacht* pogrom and sent to the Sachsenhausen concentration camp, near Berlin. During this pogrom, named 'the night of broken glass' due to the immense damage caused to property, ninety-one Jews were killed and hundreds of Jewish-owned businesses ransacked. Many more Jews committed suicide in the following weeks, dreading that the pogrom was but a prelude to further persecution. Walter was released from Sachsenhausen and subsequently able to leave Europe for the USA with Julius, thanks to the support of a cousin already living in America. In March 1939, their mother Rosa moved in with the Franks in Amsterdam.

The danger to Jews in neighbouring Germany was becoming ever more tangible, but Otto and Edith still hoped that their daughters' freedom in Amsterdam would not be compromised. Within three months of Anne's 10th birthday in June 1939, however, Europe was at war. The Nazi invasion of Poland on 1 September sparked a conflict that would endure for six years and irrevocably alter millions of lives. Approximately 30,000 German Jews had fled to the Netherlands by this time.

Life under Occupation

In the early months of the Second World War, Anne's life continued without significant change. She still had a wide circle of both Jewish and Christian friends and continued her education at the Montessori School. In spite of her somewhat frail constitution, she was an active child and enjoyed ice skating in winter and swimming in summer. She also took pleasure in acting, appearing on one occasion in a Jewish play called *The Princess with the Long Nose*. On 10 May 1940, however, Otto's belief that his family would remain safe in the Netherlands was shattered. Although the Dutch had remained neutral during the First World War, Nazi troops now marched into the country. Five days later, after the heavy bombing of Rotterdam, the Dutch surrendered. Anne was now living in an occupied country and Amsterdam quickly became the centre of Nazi activity.

Slowly at first, but with increasing regularity, the occupying Nazi forces issued anti-Jewish decrees. Otto had to officially register his family as German Jews in August 1940. In January 1941, Jews were forbidden to go to the cinema, a huge blow for Anne who loved movies and was fascinated by the glamour of Hollywood. The Dutch went on strike in February in protest against the Nazi persecution of Jews in the Netherlands, but to no avail. As spring turned to summer, Jews were no longer permitted in public swimming pools and a large black 'J' was stamped on their identity cards. The Franks officially became stateless in November 1941, losing their German nationality following a decree that revoked the citizenship of emigrants no longer living within the Reich.

It was not just Jews who were affected by changes in citizenship laws. Miep Santrouschitz, who had worked for Otto since 1933, was an Austrian national. She had lived in the Netherlands since 1920; however in 1941 she was informed that she would have to return to Vienna within three months unless she joined a club for Nazi women or married a Dutchman. She and Jan Gies already intended to marry, but this hastened their plans. Although her passport was invalidated, her uncle managed to send her birth certificate to Amsterdam, which was needed for the marriage to take place. On 16 July 1941, Anne and Otto attended Miep and Jan's wedding, a happy occasion in a year that otherwise held little promise. Margot was ill at the time, so Edith remained at home to care for both her and Oma Holländer, who was suffering from cancer. Rosa's latest operation had resulted in the postponement of Anne's birthday celebrations, so the Gies wedding must have been some small compensation. A party for the newly married couple was held in Otto's offices at 263 Prinsengracht, where Anne presented them with a silver plate. Rosa Holländer would lose her battle with cancer in January 1942.

As the Occupation wore on and the Nazis continued to introduce persecutory legislation in the Netherlands, Otto and Edith could not maintain a full sense of normalcy in their daughters' lives, or indeed continue their own daily activities as they would have wished. Otto had to aryanize his business in 1941, since as a Jew he could not hold a managerial position in a company. With assistance from his colleagues and from Jan Gies, a new company was established named 'Gies & Co' and he formally resigned as director, though unofficially remained in charge. Further legislation in September 1941 forbade all young Jews to learn alongside gentile children, therefore both Anne and Margot left their schools and began attending the Jewish Lyceum. The segregation that the family had fled in Frankfurt eight years earlier had now caught up with them in Amsterdam.

Anne's reputation for talking in class did not cease with her enrolment at the Jewish Lyceum. When set an essay on 'a chatterbox' as punishment for her repeated conversations, she argued that it was an inherited female trait and therefore she was unlikely to stop. She was swiftly set a second assignment for talking during lessons and a third when her chatter still didn't cease, which she responded to cleverly by writing her essay in verse.

At the Lyceum, Anne met Jacqueline van Maarsen, whom she singled out to be her new best friend. Although Jacque liked Anne very much, she found her quite a demanding and jealous friend at times. The two girls often stayed at each other's houses, but Anne was seldom gracious if Jacque chose to spend time with somebody else. Anne's intense curiosity about sex could be embarrassing for Jacque, who refused when Anne asked if they could touch each other's breasts as a sign of friendship. Despite Anne's extroverted, inquisitive nature, their friendship remained close.

*

From May 1942, a six-pointed yellow star bearing the label 'JOOD' (JEW) had to be sewn to all outer clothing worn by Jews in the Netherlands; a vivid label of segregation. By this time, discriminatory measures also extended to Jews not being allowed to sit on park benches, visit beaches or use the tram system. By the summer, Edith could only go shopping between the hours of three and five in the afternoon, when there was usually little fresh produce left. Similar measures were imposed across Occupied Europe, including in France and Belgium, while in countries to the east of Germany, such as Poland, 1941 saw Nazi racial policies escalate into mass murder. Mobile killing squads were deployed to annihilate people whom the Nazis considered subhuman, and among the victims were hundreds of thousands of Jews. Those who were not murdered by these *Einsatzgruppen* were crowded into ghettos, sealed off areas of cities in which poverty and disease fast became the norm.

These atrocities were as yet unknown to the Dutch, but the Jews of the Netherlands doubtless still felt their own grievances keenly. For 12 year old Anne, each Nazi decree rendered it ever harder for her and her friends to pursue the activities they had enjoyed before the Occupation. The swimming pools and skating rinks were closed to them and a curfew limited when they could venture outside their homes. Nevertheless, they still found ways to amuse themselves. Together with Jacque, Hanneli, Sanne and another friend called Ilse Wagner,

Anne was part of 'The Little Dipper Minus Two' club, named for the constellation, which met at Ilse's house to play ping-pong. The girls also visited the ice-cream parlours that still served Jewish customers, where they could usually find a male friend to purchase their ice-creams.

Though not quite a teenager, Anne enjoyed receiving attention from boys and was maturing quickly. Her parents encouraged her to enjoy as carefree a life as possible, for as her 13th birthday approached and Nazi persecution of Jews in the occupied Netherlands intensified, nobody could predict whether this relative freedom would last. Otto and Edith couldn't have known that on 20 January 1942 a meeting had taken place among fifteen senior Nazis that would have devastating consequences. In a villa on the shores of Lake Wannsee, just outside Berlin, 'the Final Solution' to the Jewish question in Europe had been discussed, setting in motion a chain of events that would result in systematic human murder on an industrial scale.

Receiving the Diary

A few days before her 13th birthday, Anne pointed out an autograph book in a shop window to her father, hinting that she would like it as a present. On 12 June 1942, this red and white chequered book was waiting for her among a pile of other gifts. She later described it as one of her nicest presents and wrote on the day she received it how she hoped it would be a source of comfort and support in which she could confide completely. In spite of the war raging across Europe, it is doubtful she knew then how poignantly prophetic these words would become, and how soon.

This autograph book immediately became Anne's diary. She wrote in detail about her birthday, including how she was allowed to choose what game her schoolmates would play. She could not join her class in their volleyball match, however, as her shoulders had a tendency to dislocate, a trick she enjoyed shocking people with throughout her childhood. Anne also celebrated turning thirteen with a party for her Jewish friends in the Merwedeplein apartment: non-Jews were no longer permitted to visit Jewish homes. A film featuring a popular dog called Rin Tin Tin was projected and she received several more gifts, greatly enjoying being the centre of attention.

In the first three weeks after she received her diary, Anne wrote predominantly about school life, her friends and the few activities that a young Jewish girl in occupied Amsterdam could still enjoy. Her descriptions of her classmates were brief, pointed and occasionally unkind, but typical of a teenager relishing in the confessional independence of writing a diary for the first time. She also wrote of her acquaintance with 16-year-old Helmuth 'Hello' Silberberg, whom she likened to a suitor. Although closer in age to Margot, who was considered the beauty of the family, Hello was struck by Anne's maturity and accompanied her on walks around the city. On one occasion Otto reproached him for bringing Anne home later than the Nazi curfew permitted, but their friendship prospered in spite of limitations the Occupation placed on their time together.

On the morning of Sunday 5 July 1942, Anne saw Hello for the last time. She was due to meet him again later that afternoon, but before he returned Margot received a call-up notice for labour service in Germany. Such notices were delivered to thousands of 15 and 16 year old German Jews on this date and although Margot initially told Anne that the summons was for their father, she soon revealed the truth, prompting her younger sister to cry. When Hello called at the Franks' apartment shortly afterwards, Edith informed him that Anne was unable to meet. Although the full objective of the Final Solution was as yet unknown, Otto and Edith had no intention of letting Margot report to the Nazi authorities and announced that the whole family would go into hiding the next day. There was very little time to prepare. Miep and Jan Gies went to Merwedeplein in the evening to take some of the Franks' belongings away, while Anne and Margot were told to gather a few possessions to carry with them in the morning. The first thing Anne packed was her diary.

Part Two: A Clandestine Existence

The Secret Annexe

Early in the morning of 6 July 1942, Miep cycled to the Franks' apartment and left quickly with Margot in tow. Margot had illegally kept her bicycle, in spite of the decree that forbade Jews from owning them, and she did not wear a yellow star as she followed Miep to an unknown destination. It was raining, a fortunate coincidence that meant there were less Nazi police patrolling Amsterdam's streets than usual.

Otto, Edith and Anne left Merwedeplein on foot, all wearing several layers of clothing beneath their coats, as to carry luggage would have aroused suspicion. Anne also did not know where they were heading, but the fact they were about to disappear was not as great a shock as it might have been. A few days before Margot's summons, Otto had casually mentioned to his youngest daughter that the family might go into hiding, assuring her that whatever happened, they would stay together. He had not divulged that he and Edith had been making preparations for months: a provisional date of 16 July had been agreed for them to move into their hiding place, but the unexpected call-up notice had hastened their plans. His attempts to procure American and then Cuban visas for his family in the early stages of the war had been unsuccessful, prompting him to make arrangements for his family to disappear.

Many Jews who went underground during the Occupation of the Netherlands ventured to countryside farmhouses, away from hubs of Nazi activity in the cities. Anne was understandably surprised when she discovered they were heading for Otto's offices at 263 Prinsengracht, in the heart of Amsterdam. The Opekta company, which specialised in a product called pectin that was used in jam-making, had moved to these premises in December 1940.

The 17th century building was located in front of the wide Prinsengracht canal and in the shadow of the Westerkerk, the city's largest Protestant church. The ground floor comprised a warehouse and business was conducted from offices on the first floor. At the rear of the building was an extension that was secluded from Amsterdam's streets by a surrounding quadrangle. This annexe, once used as a laboratory, was where Otto had decided to hide his family. It comprised four small rooms and a separate lavatory over two floors, with an attic above. The total living space was around seventy-five square metres.

Upon arrival at 263 Prinsengracht, Miep hurried a terrified Margot upstairs and pushed her through the annexe door, before retreating to the offices to commence her daily work for Opekta. When Otto, Edith and Anne arrived later, Anne saw that several pieces of furniture, substantial food supplies and many other possessions from their Merwedeplein home had already been deposited in the hiding place, which she immediately christened the Secret Annexe.

While Edith and Margot sat motionless amidst the boxes, in subdued shock, Anne and Otto set to work unpacking and organizing the small rooms. There was much to be done during the first few days and Anne initially looked upon going into hiding as an exciting adventure. She soon realised, however, that none of them knew how long it would be before they would step outside again.

Eight Jews in Hiding

The Franks lived alone in the Secret Annexe for just one week, during which most of their time was spent making the rooms tidy and habitable. On 13 July, they were joined by Hermann and Auguste van Pels and their son Peter, who at fifteen was several months younger than Margot. The van Pels family were also Jewish and had come to Amsterdam from Osnabrück in Germany in 1937; refugees by choice in search of tolerance and security. Hermann, a butcher, began working with Otto Frank in 1938. The trade in pectin was seasonal, being dependent on fruit harvests, so with his specialist knowledge of herbs and spices, Hermann brought a new means of income to the business. His family began attending the coffee afternoons hosted by Edith and Otto, who lived close by, and they soon developed a strong friendship.

During the Occupation of the Netherlands it was unusual for a whole family to stay together if they went underground, let alone for two families to live in the same hiding place. Many children were separated from their parents to live in different dwellings, or even in different towns, often moving several times as locations became unsafe or helpers untrustworthy, but this was not the case for the Frank and van Pels families. The arrangement to hide together had been made several months earlier, when Otto and Hermann decided that nobody would suspect two Jews and their families of living secretly on their own business premises in the heart of Amsterdam.

As atypical an example of a hiding place as the Secret Annexe was, it was nevertheless no small feat for seven people to reside in such a limited space. Mr and Mrs van Pels slept in the larger room on the Annexe's upper floor, which served as a kitchen and living space for everybody by day. Peter's bed was in a small adjacent area beneath the steps to the attic. The Franks slept on the lower floor, with Anne and Margot sharing the narrower of two rooms, next to the lavatory. Within a week, Anne had brightened the wall above her bed with a selection of picture postcards from her personal collection, which Otto had thoughtfully brought to the Annexe.

Initially, Anne was delighted by the arrival of the van Pelses and hoped they would all become one big family. Mrs van Pels prompted laughter on arrival by whipping a large chamber pot out of a hat box. Described by Anne as coquettish and temperamental but with a cheerful hard work ethic, she and her husband had much to tell the Franks about what had been occurring outside in the past week. They had planned to move in on July 14, but with the Nazis issuing ever more call-up notices to Jews, had decided not to delay their disappearance unduly. Indeed, the day after the van Pels family arrived in the Annexe, 962 Jews were taken from Amsterdam to the transit camp of Westerbork. On 15 July, the first train left the Netherlands for Auschwitz concentration camp, carrying 1,135 people.

Although relations between the two families were cordial at first, Anne had a bone of contention with Peter, who had brought his cat, Mouschi, to the Annexe.

As she had been forbidden to bring her own cat Moortje into hiding, this seemed a great injustice to the 13 year old. Tensions soon arose between Edith and Mrs van Pels too, as Auguste removed most of her linen supply from the communal cupboard and began making criticisms of Anne and Margot's liberal upbringing. Nevertheless, the two families continued to eat meals together and endeavoured to co-exist in their small rooms as peacefully as possible.

In November 1942, the eighth and final resident of the Secret Annexe moved in, a dentist named Fritz Pfeffer. Born in 1889, he too was a German Jew who had fled Nazi persecution in the hope of safety, along with his partner, Charlotte 'Lotte' Kaletta, a Christian lady around two decades his junior. Although the couple were deeply in love and planned to marry, the 1935 Nuremberg Laws prohibited their legal union. Fritz had a son named Werner from a previous marriage, whom he sent to live in England after the *Kristallnacht* pogrom.

As the situation for Jews in the Netherlands became more dangerous, Fritz had asked Miep, who was one of his patients, whether she knew of a safe hiding place. In the few months since the Franks and van Pelses had gone underground, call-ups had become round-ups, with Jews being taken away directly from their homes instead of receiving summons instructing them to report to the station. It had been agreed in the Annexe that where seven could eat, so could eight and thus on 16 November Dr Pfeffer arrived. He had known the Franks for several years and was surprised to find them alive and well in central Amsterdam, as a false trail had led him, like many others, to believe they had escaped to Switzerland.

Indeed, when Hannah Goslar discovered that Anne had disappeared, after knocking on the front door to borrow Edith's kitchen scales, their tenant informed her that the family had probably gone to Switzerland.

The sleeping arrangements were altered in light of Pfeffer's arrival: Margot moved in to her parents' room and Anne gained a 53-year-old male room-mate. She was again initially positive about the addition to the Annexe family, but as 1942 drew to a close, it was clear that with eight people living in such confined quarters, tensions and quarrels would be unavoidable.

Daily Life in the Annexe

Visits from Miep and the other office staff who knew about the hidden Jews were greatly anticipated in the Annexe: not only did their presence bring variety to the company, it also heralded the hours when words could be spoken instead of whispered, tip-toeing in socks was no longer imperative and the toilet could be flushed. Life was strictly governed by the office working hours and the nearby bells of the Westerkerk clock chiming every quarter hour ensured that everybody in the Annexe was always aware of the time. Anne, in particular, found these bells reassuring, and was dismayed when they stopped ringing in August 1943. Curtains were drawn across all windows during the day, imposing an imperfect and omnipresent gloom, and blackouts were put up at night.

To have a lavatory and sink inside a hiding place was a luxury, although water could not be run during the working day. Adhering to a strict routine enabled everybody to wash before the staff arrived downstairs. At weekends, each person had their own preferred space for taking a bath. After some deliberation, Anne chose the office lavatory as her bathing territory. Venturing into the offices when the staff were absent allowed the eight Jews a little more space and privacy than was possible in the seventy-five square metres of the Annexe. Rigorous exercise was naturally denied to them, but they did endeavour to undertake light calisthenics and thus maintain some level of physical activity.

Meals were eaten at regular times to coincide with when the office staff arrived, took their lunch, and left the building. Mrs van Pels presided over much of the cooking, sharing the housewifely duties with Edith Frank. In a humorous prospectus written by the van Pels family before Fritz Pfeffer moved in to the Annexe, breakfast, lunch, dinner and rest hours were all meticulously outlined, with Sundays and public holidays representing the only exceptions to the rigid routine. This homemade pamphlet also contained details about radio broadcasts and stipulated that no German should be spoken, despite the fact that many of the adults struggled with the Dutch language. Classical German literature and music was nevertheless permitted, indeed, Anne was encouraged by Otto, himself a keen reader, to read works by well-known German writers.

The Frank sisters often assisted their mother and Mrs van Pels with mealtime preparations and cleaning, although occasionally the whole Annexe family would be enrolled in culinary tasks such as peeling potatoes, shelling peas, or rubbing beans to rid them of mould. Meals became smaller and less varied as the war impacted on supplies outside, but unsatisfactory dinners seemed a small price for living in relative safety. It was vital that everyone remained healthy, as visiting or calling a doctor would have been impossible. At one point there was much discussion over whether Anne needed glasses, but although the family deliberated seriously over whether Miep could accompany the young teenager to have her eyes tested, it was ultimately decided that the risk of going outside was too great.

Otto, who assumed something of a leadership role within the group, decreed that everyone should live by the motto *fac et spera*: work and hope. The obligatory silence during weekdays was conducive to study and everyone had their own areas of interest. Anne's favourite subjects included mythology, history and genealogy, with a particular passion for royal family trees. Alongside the pictures of film stars she pasted on her bedroom wall were postcards of the English princesses, Elizabeth and Margaret. Although studying for pleasure was instilled in both Anne and Margot, Otto insisted that Anne also pursued areas she was less fond of, such as mathematics. The Frank sisters applied themselves diligently under Otto's tutelage and often undertook additional office tasks for Miep and her colleague Bep Voskuijl, which gave them a sense of purpose. Peter was less academically inclined than the two girls, but also studied English and French under Otto's guidance. He often spent time in the attic, where he built himself a small workshop and enjoyed developing his carpentry skills

Besides personal study, reading, board games and knitting were all ways in which the silent hours were passed. Most evenings, the eight Jews trooped downstairs to the office, where they listened to BBC radio broadcasts from the exiled Dutch government in London. Knowledge of the war's progress brought both joy and despair, but vitally provided new fuel for conversation. As weeks became months, the composed Franks and mercurial van Pelses became exasperated with each other's company, even within the family factions, and argued frequently over finances and the division of food. Although generally a jovial man who often regaled the Annexe family with jokes, Hermann van Pels nevertheless became short-tempered as his cigarette supplies ran low and had blazing rows with his wife over whether her clothes and jewellery should be sold to fund household necessities. The outspoken Anne clashed particularly frequently with Pfeffer, whom she considered stern, stubborn and old-fashioned. She apparently never knew that he had a son and their relationship was fraught within weeks of his arrival, probably deriving as much from their forty-year age gap as from the strains of living in confined quarters.

Margot and Peter, though also teenagers, were usually far less involved in the Annexe conflicts than Anne. Naturally more sedate and retiring than her sister, Margot seems to have become completely withdrawn during the twenty-five months spent in hiding. She studied and read extensively, taking external courses in Latin and stenography, in addition to pursuing subjects ranging from trigonometry and geometry to bookkeeping and economics. She also assisted the older Annexe members with their Dutch, often correcting letters for Pfeffer. With a few exceptions, it seems Peter was also seldom at the forefront of any activity. Anne recorded a dispute he had with his parents over a forbidden book and also wrote about an evening when she and Peter dressed up to the great amusement of everyone else; she in male clothing and he in his mother's dress. Otherwise, he received little attention in Anne's diary until 1944.

Despite moments of discord and clashes of personality, birthdays were always celebrated, as were events such as Hanukkah and even St Nicholas' Day, a Christian festival which the Franks had never marked before 1942. The hidden Jews and their helpers exchanged small gifts and the Franks created humorous poems for each other, as was their family tradition. Any excuse to vary the daily routine was pounced upon, whether a holiday, watching Mr van Pels make sausages after a delivery of meat, or assisting Pfeffer with dental checks. Anne recorded all these aspects of clandestine life in her diary, from the frustration of enforced silence and rigid routine, to contrasting moments of amusement and fear.

The Helpers

When Otto had first considered going into hiding, he knew it would be impossible without help from gentile friends. At the most basic level, how could four people survive an indeterminate length of time shut inside, without someone to purchase and bring them food and drink? Miep did not hesitate to say yes when he asked if she would accept responsibility for looking after his family in hiding, and Jan similarly proffered his assistance. Johannes Kleiman, who had known Otto since the 1920s and worked with him as a bookkeeper for several years, actually suggested the empty rooms in the annexe as a suitable hiding place and assisted with preparing the space for habitation. The other key office staff, Victor Kugler and Bep Voskuijl, were also informed that the Franks would be living secretly at 263 Prinsengracht. All accepted this perilous responsibility willingly, fully conscious that even the knowledge of Jews in hiding placed them at risk, let alone the dangers inherent in actively assisting their friends, as under Nazi law it was illegal to shelter Jews.

Miep's role centred on providing the Annexe residents with food. Since all produce was rationed in the Netherlands during the war, Jan purchased additional food and clothing coupons through underground resistance networks. In early 1942, Mr van Pels had regularly taken Miep to visit a fellow butcher on a street close to the Opekta premises. She had not understood the reason for these excursions, but when she later visited this butcher alone, after her friends had moved into the Annexe, he always gave her what extra meat he could, recognising, no doubt, that she was now supporting Hermann van Pels. A local grocer, Mr van Hoeve, also set aside a little extra for Miep whenever he could and carried sacks of potatoes to Prinsengracht, suspecting that she was providing for people who could not shop themselves.

Bep Voskuijl, born in 1919, had worked at Opekta as a typist since 1937. She took the daily supply of milk to the Annexe and often ate lunch with the two families and Pfeffer. She also submitted Margot's Latin exercises to an external tutor under her own name, allowing Margot to progress in her studies. Like Miep, Jan and the other Opekta employees who cared for the eight Jews, Bep knew that her friendship and knowledge of the outside world were valued just as much as her practical assistance. Whenever one of the helpers entered the Annexe, they were instantly bombarded with questions, especially by inquisitive Anne. As the youngest helper, Bep was particularly close to Anne and the two often shared whispered conversations.

Bep's father, Johan Voskuijl, managed the Opekta warehouse and also knew about the hidden Jews. In mid-August 1942, he constructed a wooden bookcase to mask the Annexe entrance, enhancing security. It swung forward on special hinges and as Anne remarked in her diary, made their hiding place feel truly secret. When Mr Voskuijl later had to leave his job due to stomach cancer, this induced great unease among the hidden Jews, as the newly appointed warehouse manager,

Willem van Maaren, was extremely curious about the rooms at the back of the building.

Mr Kleiman and Mr Kugler assumed responsibility for the financial side of caring for people who could not openly earn a living. Sales were made without being recorded so that money could be passed directly to Otto, who discussed the business with Kleiman and Kugler daily, effectively maintaining some level of managerial input. Despite the outside presentation of a fully aryanized business, he had continued to work in the office whenever possible, though his hours had been steadily dwindling. Kleiman was also able, in business correspondence to Erich Elias, to subtly infer that the Franks were safe and being cared for, though Leni and her family never guessed the truth or magnitude of his involvement. Although Kleiman maintained a cheerful exterior, and was described by Edith as always bringing sunshine into the room, the Annexe residents and other helpers knew he was suffering with health problems, in particular stomach ulcers. The stress of the responsibility he bore cannot have helped and in 1943 he underwent surgery for gastric bleeding. Kugler, also under immense pressure, never told his wife that he was helping to protect hidden Jews.

At Anne's request, Miep and Jan spent a night in the Annexe on 19 October 1942. Anne typed a special menu for them, as guests of honour, and was delighted to give Miep her bed as she and Margot slept in their parents' room. Miep could not sleep, however, and later recalled the sense of oppression and fear she felt in the silent house. Bep also stayed in the Annexe overnight on one occasion and was similarly unnerved by the experience.

Fritz Pfeffer's arrival made further overnight stays impractical, but the helpers continued to visit daily and share lunchtime meals with the eight Jews.

In addition to necessities such as foodstuffs, the helpers also provided fresh supplies of reading material. Kugler bought Anne *Cinema* & *Theatre* magazine every Monday to feed her passion for movie news and Miep carried library books to the Annexe on a weekly basis. She also ferried letters between Pfeffer and Lotte Kaletta, although Lotte never suspected that Miep was so actively involved in helping her partner, nor that he was hiding in the city. In spite of the great emotional stress of caring for eight people and keeping their presence secret, to say nothing of the challenging practicalities, the helpers never complained and did their utmost to make life as bearable as they could for their charges. Unknown to the Franks or Pfeffer, on Miep Gies' birthday in February 1944, Mrs van Pels drew her aside and presented her with an antique ring made of diamond and onyx, as a means of expressing her gratitude.

Constant Fear: Bombs and Burglaries

Although a routine of work and study provided temporary distraction for the eight Jews, it was often impossible to alleviate the fear of discovery or destruction. Amsterdam was bombed several times during the war and in 263 Prinsengracht, planes could clearly be heard flying overhead. There was a very real possibility that the Annexe might be hit and Anne frequently ran to her father's bed when the guns sounded in the night. On one occasion, Otto refused to put on a light despite his daughter's frightened pleas, fearing that somebody outside would be alerted to their presence. Edith lit a candle, however, reproaching Otto for his lack of sympathy and remarking that unlike him, Anne was not an ex-soldier.

At times when the rest of the building was empty and the bombs were falling, Anne ran up and down stairs in an attempt to alleviate her fears and subjugate the noise of gunfire. She was by no means alone in her discomfort, and Mrs van Pels in particular would panic during these bombardments. Speculation over the best course of action in the event of a fire or flood was a regular topic of discussion, though beyond having an emergency bag ready, it is not known whether there was ever a concrete plan as to what they would have done in the case of having to evacuate their hiding place. Edith found the situation of being in hiding extremely depressing. Miep later recalled how, unbeknown to her companions, Edith would accompany her to the Annexe door then confess her feelings of despair, remarking that she could not foresee a positive end to the war.

In addition to the threat of bombs, the Annexe residents knew only too well what fate might befall them should they be discovered. Radio reports of Jews being gassed to death in Poland had not escaped them, reluctant though they were to accept the truth of such stories. In November 1943, Anne dreamed that her friend Hannah Goslar was in a concentration camp, clothed in rags. This had a profound effect on her and she lamented the selfish way in which she believed she had treated her friend, praying that Hanneli would be spared from suffering. At this time Hannah was, in fact, in the Westerbork transit camp, having been sent there with her father, sister and grandparents following a mass round up in June.

The fear of capture was heightened following several break-ins at 263 Prinsengracht in 1943 and 1944, and compounded by moments of carelessness. On one occasion in March 1943, the Annexe family had left chairs grouped around the private office wireless, which was still illegally tuned to the BBC. Later, financial concerns were raised when Hermann van Pels left his wallet in the ground floor warehouse one evening, from which his last hundred guilder note was stolen. The empty wallet was given to Victor Kugler by the warehouse staff, who were suspicious as to whom it belonged and about how it had appeared in the building overnight.

In April 1944, burglars kicked a hole in the warehouse door and it is possible that Mr van Pels, who went to investigate, was actually seen by the intruders and alerted them to the internal presence. The eight Jews spent a fearful night in silence on this occasion, clustered on the Annexe's upper floor with only a wastebasket in which to relieve themselves. Later that night police explored the building and rattled the bookcase, leading a terrified Anne to believe that discovery was imminent. After minutes of suspense the police retreated, but everyone knew how lucky they had been to escape detection.

Following this incident, Jan decreed that none of them should venture down to the offices after hours, especially if they suspected an unwelcome presence in the building. Burglars were as unpredictable as bombs, and for Jews in hiding in a Nazi-occupied country, the consequences could be equally as devastating.

An Isolated Adolescence

For adolescent Anne, who had so enjoyed the variety and freedom of city life, living in enforced isolation from the outside world for an indeterminate length of time was extremely testing. It exacerbated the natural confusions and frustrations of puberty and the youngest Annexe resident wrote about her feelings in her diary with increasing introspection.

Throughout the period in hiding, Anne's relationship with her sister fluctuated between frustration and friendship, with Anne often commenting on Margot's apparently superior intellect, goodwill and beauty, but as time drew on she did record moments of sisterly intimacy with more regularity. She mentioned that Margot, too, wrote a diary, but no trace of her older sister's personal writing has ever been found.

More tangible than Anne's friction with Margot was the conflict she experienced with her mother. She had always been a self-confessed Daddy's girl, idolizing Pim, but in the close quarters of the Annexe, Edith keenly felt the preferential treatment her spouse received from their youngest daughter. Anne was undoubtedly harsh towards her mother, frequently criticizing Edith for her perceived lack of compassion, although she did later temper some of her more virulent diary outbursts on the subject of Edith's parenting. She had often commented, for example on her mother's sarcasm and lack of tact, but later acknowledged that she had not understood her mother. Indeed, it seems Edith often defended her youngest daughter when she came under criticism from Mr and Mrs van Pels, who were frequently disparaging on the subjects of eating habits and how children should be raised, and did her utmost to maintain a positive relationship with Anne, even when she was dismissive and tempestuous.

Anne was in many ways a mature teenager, but felt she was very much treated as the baby of the Annexe, a fact she resented intensely. Certain books were denied to her and it was testing for a 13-year-old girl to share a tiny room with a middle-aged man. The desk in their room was the object of intense discord when Pfeffer rejected Anne's request to work there for longer than ninety minutes a day, claiming that a teenager's projects were unimportant compared to his own academic pursuits. Only after Otto's diplomatic intervention was Anne permitted to use the desk for two full afternoons a week.

Anne started her first menstrual cycle in hiding and underwent a significant growth spurt. Otto regularly measured his daughters against the wall, marking their heights in pencil, and between September 1942 and July 1944, Anne grew 13 centimetres. The last time she was measured she was 1.68m tall – about five feet six inches. Chairs had to be added to the end of the bed on which she slept and she rapidly outgrew the clothes she had brought with her to the Annexe. Without a friend in whom to confide, she poured her thoughts into her diary, writing candidly about her physical development and emotional experiences of puberty.

Although there were no opportunities to socialise, Anne took great pride in her appearance even when clothes no longer fitted properly, curling her hair every night and bleaching the hairs on her upper lip. Miep, sensing that the developing girl needed to feel attractive, found a pair of second-hand red shoes with heels when shopping and presented them to Anne as a surprise. They fitted perfectly and Anne was delighted.

In early 1944, Anne dreamed about Peter Schiff, an older boy she had loved at school. Thereafter she began spending time with Peter van Pels, whose company she had not sought before, but who now became a close friend. Anne was longing for freedom, independence and companionship and in the confines of the Annexe, this relationship with Peter quickly developed an intensity neither had previously experienced. They discussed matters ranging from sex and religion to their imperfect relationships with their parents, spending time in the attic where they could look out of the window at the sky. It was Anne who determined the course of the relationship, coaxing Peter from his usual state of quiet withdrawal. As she confided in him, he opened up to her and in April 1944 the two shared a first kiss, leading to many subsequent embraces.

Otto, fully aware of the blossoming friendship, cautioned Anne to be sensible, whereupon she wrote him a letter asserting her independence and asking to be left alone. The aftermath was a hurt father and a remorseful daughter. Anne respected her parents' authority, but like most girls of fourteen, desperately wanted to feel some sense of autonomy over her life. Her extraordinary circumstances allowed few opportunities for independence and she continued to visit Peter in the attic, albeit with a somewhat tempered ardour. This romantic episode, though undoubtedly innocent by 21st century standards, would become one of the aspects of Anne's diary that later most intrigued and moved readers.

Shut inside, Anne was not only missing varied company and friendship. She described her growing longing for nature and fresh air, admiring the chestnut tree that stood outside the attic window. She pondered deeply on religion and articulated her faith in God on numerous occasions. Although Peter became a great support, Anne's infatuation with him waned as she realized they shared different religious values and that he lacked ambition, in stark contrast to her own outlook. As the war continued through the spring of 1944, she increasingly devoted herself to writing, dedicating more time to her diary and also creating short fairy stories. Around this time, Anne decided she wanted to make writing a career in later life. She also had ambitions to travel to London and Paris, to attain Dutch citizenship, and study art history. While she was candid in her wish to marry and have children, she did not want to follow in her mother's footsteps and become a housewife with no other calling, aspiring instead to make what she hoped would be a tangible difference in the world.

Imprisoned in the same, cramped environment for months on end, with no outlet for her teenage anxieties and sorrows, it is unsurprising that Anne's diary became her greatest source of comfort and companionship. She felt unable to express her deeper feelings around the adults, whom she believed saw only the vain, outspoken side of her character, and so committed her contemplations to paper.

Rewriting the Diary

On 28 March 1944, an idea was planted in Anne's mind that gave her a new sense of purpose. The Annexe family was listening, as usual, to the exiled Dutch government's Radio Oranje broadcast. Gerrit Bolkestein, the Education Minister, suggested that after the war, a collection should be made of diaries and letters to show how the Dutch had suffered during the Occupation. Everyone in the Annexe knew that Anne kept a diary and immediately remarked on its suitability should such an archive be established.

Anne reflected on how interesting a novel called *Het Achterhuis* (*The Annexe*) would appear to prospective readers once the war was finished. In early April she wrote about her desire to become a journalist and the joy and comfort she found in expressing herself through writing. In addition to her diary and some short fictional stories, she had completed several humorous sketches about Annexe life. She had asked Kleiman to submit some of her work to a magazine, but even under a different name he thought it would be too great a risk. Undeterred, on 11 May Anne decided her diary would serve as a sound basis for a novel about the Secret Annexe and soon afterwards began the involved task of revising nearly two years' worth of entries, with a view to post-war publication.

From 1942, Anne had written her diary in the form of letters, addressing them to numerous female characters from Cissy van Marxveldt's *Joop ter Heul* book series for adolescent girls, which she greatly admired. She also wrote two letters to Jacqueline van Maarsen, bidding her farewell and promising to always stay best friends. Soon, however, she wrote uniquely to a character called Kitty and it appears that Anne intended her novel to be written as diary letters to this particular 'friend'.

As Anne began re-writing her diary as *Het Achterhuis*, she added sections from memory, combined certain entries, and made omissions where she felt content was too banal or personal. She integrated some of her sketches about the Annexe and also created pseudonyms for her 'characters'. The Frank family became the Robin family and Hermann, Auguste and Peter van Pels became Hans, Petronella and Alfred van Daan. Her choice of name for Dr Pfeffer was Albert Dussel, which is indicative of her growing animosity with her roommate as from German, Dussel loosely translates as nitwit. The helpers were also assigned different names: Miep and Jan became Anne and Henk van Santen; Bep was Elli Vossen; and Kugler and Kleiman were, respectively, Harry Kraler and Simon Koophuis.

The chequered autograph book that Anne received for her 13th birthday had been full since December 1942. She continued her diary entries in notebooks, but for the revisions worked on thin sheets of coloured paper supplied to her by Miep and Bep. Between May and August, Anne revised her original diary entries from 12 June 1942 to 29 March 1944, covering 324 sheets of paper in this time. While working intently upon her *Achterhuis*, she continued keeping her usual diary, recording events with increasing flair and fluency. She read broadly throughout the twenty-five months in hiding, which may have lent itself to her progressively confident writing style. The intense longings and frustrations she felt from early 1944 onwards were eloquently described in a literary style that few would have recognised as flowing from the pen of a 14 year old.

On 1 August 1944, six weeks after her fifteenth birthday, Anne wrote to Kitty for the last time.

Part Three: The Final Solution

The Arrest: 4 August 1944

On the morning of Friday 4 August 1944, a car drew up outside 263 Prinsengracht. Several men exited the vehicle and made their way inside, among them an Austrian officer named Karl Josef Silberbauer and some members of the Dutch Nazi Party. They had been tipped off that Jews were hiding on the premises.

These men were pointed towards the first floor offices by the warehouse staff. Upon entering, a pistol was drawn and Kugler was ordered to show Silberbauer where the Jews were hiding. Unwillingly, Kugler took the men to the bookcase. After twenty-five months of perpetual trepidation, for both the Jews in hiding and their protectors, the game was up.

Otto was giving Peter an English lesson when the Nazis entered the Annexe and they were the last to realise that their hiding place had been discovered. Stunned, they joined their families and Pfeffer on the lower floor, where they were ordered to give up their valuables. Looking for something in which to transport the loot, Silberbauer picked up Otto's leather briefcase, the private place Anne had chosen to keep her diaries and revisions. Her writings were unceremoniously emptied on the floor and the little cash the Franks still had was stashed away by the Gestapo.

Initially, the Jews were told they had just a few minutes to each pack a small bag before departure, but Silberbauer then saw Otto's trunk, evidently the property of a German war veteran. He was astonished that this Jew had served in the German army and subsequently told everyone to take their time. Similarly astounding was Otto's revelation that they had been in hiding for over two years. As proof, Silberbauer was shown the pencil lines where Otto had charted Anne and Margot's growth since 1942 and a map studded with colourful pins, charting the progress of the invasion. D-Day, on 6 June 1944, had been jubilantly celebrated in the Annexe, as they had believed that the liberation could not be far away. Anne and Margot had even hoped that they might be able to return to school later in the year. Now, however, it was evident that for all of them, the Allied invasion had begun too late.

One by one, Anne, Margot, Otto, Edith, Mr and Mrs van Pels, Peter and Pfeffer were marched downstairs to transport waiting on the street. None of them had stepped outside since 1942. It was a crime to shelter Jews and Kugler and Kleiman were also arrested. Bep managed to leave the premises without arousing suspicion while Miep warned Jan away at lunchtime, pushing their friends' ration coupons into his hands. Jan left swiftly and later watched from across the canal as the Franks, van Pelses, Pfeffer, Kleiman and Kugler were driven away in a truck. He then informed Lotte Kaletta that her partner had been arrested.

Miep remained at her desk following an altercation with Silberbauer, who suspected her involvement but did not arrest her due to their shared Viennese heritage. He passed the keys of the building to Willem van Maaren, the warehouseman.

The prisoners from 263 Prinsengracht were taken through Amsterdam to the Nazi headquarters at Euterpestraat, where they were interrogated. Naturally, they could not divulge any information about where other Jews might be found, as they had been cut off from the outside world for so long. Kugler and Kleiman were then moved to jail on Amstelveensweg and later to the Amersfoort concentration camp, while the eight Jews were taken to cells in the Weteringschans prison.

Westerbork and Deportation

On 8 August 1944, after four nights in prison cells, the Franks, van Pelses and Pfeffer were taken to Amsterdam's Centraal station. Here, they were put on a train to Westerbork, a transit camp in northern Holland. Although they were seated in ordinary passenger cars, the doors were bolted. Anne spent much of the journey staring out of the window at the passing countryside.

Westerbork had been established as a transit camp for Jews in 1942. In many ways it was like a small town, with its own school, hospital and shops. Anne and her family were placed in the punishment barracks and given overalls with a red patch to denote their criminal status. As Jews who had been in hiding, failing to comply with the Nazi authorities, they were considered convicts. The women had to sleep separately from the men, but the Franks could be together in the evenings when the working day was over.

Otto tried to find Anne work in the toilets so she could be nearer to him in the day, but without success. Instead she had to break up batteries, as did her mother and Margot, a duty that was particularly unpleasant due to dust that was created from separating the components. Nevertheless, the women assigned to this work were at least permitted to talk. Anne briefly fell ill in Westerbork, but eyewitness recollections of her time in the camp indicate that she was generally cheerful and hopeful, often spending time with Peter van Pels as well as her father in the evenings.

Since the summer of 1942, transports had left Westerbork regularly for Nazi concentration camps, usually on Tuesdays and Fridays. By September 1944, over 100,000 Jews had been deported from Westerbork to Auschwitz, Sobibor, Theresienstadt and Bergen-Belsen. Each time the finalized lists detailing who would leave Westerbork were announced, chaos and fear reigned in the camp, as people desperately tried to alter their circumstances. Such endeavours were futile.

On Saturday 2 September 1944, 1,019 names were read out of people who were to leave Westerbork the next day. The eight Jews who had lived safely in the Secret Annexe for so long were all on this list. The next morning, just over four weeks after her arrival in Westerbork, Anne climbed into a cattle car with her family. Over seventy people were crammed into each car of the train and the doors were bolted behind them. There were no windows and no seats. The only provisions were one pail in which people could relieve themselves and another that contained water. This was one of the last transports to leave Westerbork.

For three days and nights, the train travelled eastwards across Nazi-Occupied Europe, stopping occasionally but never letting the people on board exit the cattle cars in which they were imprisoned. The stench from so many people locked in one small space was soon overwhelming and with barely any food or water, some died on the journey.

Anne and her family, like everyone else, could neither sit down nor lie down. Edith unpicked the red patches that had been sewn to their overalls, thinking they might receive better treatment if they were not seen to be criminals. Anne and Margot leaned against their parents in the hope of sleep. They knew they were heading east, but could not say when or where this nightmare journey would end.

On the night of 5-6 September, the train reached its destination: Auschwitz-Birkenau concentration camp in Poland.

Two Months in Auschwitz

Auschwitz, in southern Poland, had begun operating in 1940, originally housing political prisoners. In addition to being a labour camp, as the war progressed it also became an extermination centre; the only camp in the Nazi system with this dual purpose, and the largest. The Nazis deliberately arranged for transports to reach concentration camps in the dark, as it increased the prisoners' disorientation. Such was the case with the Westerbork transport and as its cattle cars were unbolted, the exhausted occupants were ordered on to the Auschwitz platform. Men and women were immediately, forcefully separated beneath glaring lights and this was the last time that Anne saw her beloved Pim. The distress and shock of their parting was experienced by thousands.

The sick, the elderly and children under sixteen were generally sent straight to the gas chambers upon arrival at Auschwitz. Convoys of Jewish deportees arriving at the camp had been subject to this selection process from 1942 and of the 1,019 people on the same transport as the Franks, 549 were murdered within hours. Anne must have been perceived as older than she was, or at least as being fit and healthy enough to work, as she was not selected for this fate and was instead marched to Birkenau, the women's camp. Had the Franks been sent to Sobibor, a smaller extermination camp where several other transports from Westerbork went, it is likely that they all would have been gassed shortly after arrival. Auschwitz was a hell on earth, but the selection process meant there was at least a chance of survival. Of the 34,000 Dutch Jews sent to Sobibor, however, only 19 survived.

Along with Edith, Margot and the other women who were not immediately killed, Anne was subjected to the humiliating process of disinfection. She was ordered to undress and herded into a communal shower. The dark curly hair of which she was so proud was shaved from her head and hair from her armpits and genital region was also removed. Like everyone who entered Auschwitz as a labourer, she was tattooed with a number on her left arm. Anne's exact number is not known, as the Nazis destroyed many of their records, but it would have been between A-25060 and A-25271.

Anne, Margot and Edith were placed in Women's Block 29. Over 1,000 women were housed in this barracks, which was filled with narrow, three-tiered wooden bunks. There was no heating in these buildings; at best prisoners could expect a thin blanket and possibly a straw mattress. Eyewitness reports suggest that whatever tensions existed between the three women in hiding, all were forgotten upon entering Auschwitz-Birkenau. Separated from Otto, mother and daughters formed a close trio, intent on supporting each other and remaining together.

Each morning and evening, regardless of the weather, inmates were made to stand at *Zählappel* (roll call), in rows of five. Morning roll calls could start as early as three or four o'clock. As they were counted and recounted, often for several hours, many people collapsed from exhaustion, whereupon the whole process would begin again. After the roll call was finally complete, the working day began. Anne's exact duties are unknown, but it is likely that she was assigned to hard labour tasks such as digging earth or moving rocks. Food rations in Auschwitz were minimal and prisoners were not expected to prosper in the harsh environment into which they were thrust.

Due to the lice that infested the camp and the impossibility of maintaining personal cleanliness, Anne developed an infectious skin condition and was sent to the *Krätze* (scabies) block. Margot voluntarily went with her so she would not be alone. Edith pushed what little food she could acquire to her daughters through a hole in the ground, assisted by other women with whom she had become acquainted. During this time several other women they knew, the majority of whom survived the war, were transported to another labour camp, but Margot and Edith refused to leave Anne behind and so all three remained in Birkenau.

Death was omnipresent in Auschwitz. People threw themselves against the electrified wire fences in despair, were routinely beaten or shot by Nazi guards, or simply collapsed from weakness, never to stand again. The crematoria furnaces burned steadily and every inmate knew that the smallest sign of frailty during a selection could be a death warrant. Fear of being sent to the gas chambers, or to the infamous Dr Josef Mengele for medical experimentation, was constant. Survivors of Auschwitz later recalled the horror of realising what the smoking chimneys and accompanying stench represented, even though their instincts fought to repress the knowledge of deliberate human annihilation.

After nearly two months in the camp, probably on 28 October 1944, Anne and Margot were selected for a transport. The Nazis knew the Russians were advancing towards Germany and planned to steadily eradicate traces of what had occurred in Auschwitz, in part by moving a large percentage of the concentration camp populace westwards. Edith, powerless to challenge the decision, was left alone in Birkenau, not knowing where her daughters were going, whether she would ever see them again, or if her husband was still alive. She escaped a selection for the gas chambers soon after Anne and Margot were transported, but became increasingly ill, suffering from grief, hunger and exhaustion. In the hospital, she saved every scrap of food she could find beneath her blanket, telling other women that she was keeping it for her daughters and refusing to eat anything herself. She died on 6 January 1945, ten days before her 45th birthday and three weeks before Auschwitz was liberated by the Russians.

Alone in Bergen-Belsen

Bergen-Belsen was situated on the Lüneberg Heath in Germany. Originally a transit camp, inmates were not systematically destroyed as they were in the gas chambers of Auschwitz and for this reason there was a perception that survival here would be easier. However, Belsen was not intended to hold the volume of prisoners that entered its gates in late 1944. When Anne and Margot arrived in the camp in early November, after another nightmare journey, tents had been erected to try and house the latest influx of prisoners. A violent storm several days later caused several of these tents to collapse and chaos ensued, with many people suffocating beneath the canvas.

Anne and Margot survived this incident and made friends with Janny Brandes-Brilleslijper and Lientje Rebling-Brilleslijper, two Dutch sisters they had first met in Westerbork and alongside whom they now worked, dismantling shoes by hand. The small group sang songs at Hanukkah and endeavoured to maintain a sense of hope as a desolate winter set in and provisions became increasingly scarce. The Frank sisters were also reunited with Auguste van Pels in Bergen-Belsen, who nursed Margot when she became ill, but it is not known how long she remained with them, as she was transported elsewhere sometime in early 1945.

Hannah Goslar had been in Belsen since February 1944. In early 1945, she heard that her friend Anne

Frank was in another part of the camp. Thanks to Mrs van Pels, the two girls established contact through the barbed wire fence, although they could not see each other as it was packed with straw. Hanneli was shocked to hear her distraught friend for the first time in nearly three years, as she had believed the Franks to be safe in Switzerland. Anne told her that both her parents were dead and that she and Margot were ill and had no food. Evidently, the sisters believed that Edith had been selected and that Otto, as an older man, had been gassed on his arrival at Auschwitz.

Unlike Anne, Hannah received Red Cross packages and after gathering a few items together she threw a small bundle over the fence, hoping it would give the Frank sisters some sustenance. Anne cried in frustration that another woman had caught the package and run away. On a subsequent meeting, however, Anne caught another little parcel that Hannah had gathered for her. This was the last contact between the two friends, believed to be sometime in February. Hannah's father died shortly thereafter, but she and her sister Gabi were evacuated from the camp in early April and eventually liberated by Russian troops.

Disease was rife in Belsen and in the appallingly unhygienic conditions, Anne and Margot contracted typhus, which affects both mind and body. They were already severely emaciated and demoralized, believing they had only each other to live for. The only discord between the sisters manifested itself through their illness, which caused them to squabble occasionally as their health deteriorated. Anne, suffering from terrible hallucinations, threw all her clothes away due to her horror of lice. Janny Brandes-Brilleslijper found her wrapped in only a blanket and managed to find her something else to wear, but Anne was now seriously ill, as was Margot.

The two sisters found a space in one of the camp barracks, but it was unfortunately located close to the entrance, meaning they were continually subjected to the freezing winter winds. The winter of 1944-45 was an especially harsh one and with minimal protection against the elements and barely any nourishment, there was little they could do to withstand the cold. As typhus took increasing hold of Anne and Margot, their voices became steadily weaker as they shouted at the other women to shut the door.

Margot reportedly fell from her bed to the floor of the barracks. The shock was too much for her frail body and she never got up again. She may have just reached her 19th birthday, but the exact date of her death is unknown. Anne, sick, starving and alone, succumbed to the disease within days of her sister. She was 15 years old. Although the Red Cross later recorded their deaths as being 31 March 1945, recent research that takes into account survivor testimonies and the medical onset of typhus suggests it is far more likely that Anne and Margot perished sometime during the month of February. Their bodies were dumped in a mass grave, just two people among tens of thousands who died in the camp in the final months of the war.

Bergen-Belsen was liberated by the Allies on 15 April 1945. In the following weeks thousands more prisoners succumbed to death, too weak to recover, and over 20,000 victims were interred in purpose-dug pits.

Otto's Return

After being separated from his wife and daughters upon arrival at Auschwitz in September 1944, Otto Frank had not, as Anne had assumed, been sent to the gas chamber. Although in his mid-fifties, he looked reasonably robust and was permitted entry to the camp as a labourer, as were Fritz Pfeffer and Hermann and Peter van Pels.

Hermann van Pels was the first of the Annexe residents to be killed, sometime in October 1944. According to eyewitnesses, including Otto Frank, he injured his hand whilst working and asked to be moved inside, although he knew the risks of being among weaker inmates should a selection be carried out. His luck failed when this barracks was emptied the next day and he was gassed to death, mere weeks before the gas chambers were dismantled.

Fritz Pfeffer remained with the other men from the Annexe until he was transferred to Neuengamme camp in Germany, probably via Sachsenhausen. His death from enterocolitis, a disease of the intestine, was recorded on 20 December 1944 – whether this is indeed how he died is unknown. His partner Lotte only found out that he would not be returning home in late 1945. Peter van Pels remained with Otto, who later reminisced that he was like a son to him at this time, and managed to get a job in the camp's post office. Although Otto became sick and weak, ending up in the hospital, he did not succumb to his illness.

In January 1945, the Nazis knew the Russians were drawing ever-closer to Auschwitz and hurriedly began mass evacuations of the camp, forcing thousands of skeletal prisoners westwards into the Reich. Peter, in relatively good health, thought he would have a better chance of survival if he went on a so-called death march, despite Otto's wishes that they remain together. He left Auschwitz in mid-January. Despite the harsh winter conditions and the strenuous march, Peter's strength held out for nearly four more months. He died in Mauthausen concentration camp in Austria on 5 May 1945, the same day it was liberated. He was 18 years old.

Otto, too weak to leave with Peter, remained in the Auschwitz hospital. He was liberated by the Russians on 27 January 1945 and slowly repatriated to Amsterdam, a stateless man, via Odessa and Marseilles. On this journey he learned of Edith's death from one of the women who had cared for her in Auschwitz. He was also able to write to his mother in Switzerland for the first time since 1942, informing her that he was alive, but that he had no knowledge of his daughters' whereabouts. These communications did not arrive in Basle for many months and one can only imagine the shock his family endured on receiving them. Leni had heard nothing from her brother since a cryptic postcard sent on 6 July 1942, the day the family had gone into hiding, which wished her a happy birthday months in advance and hinted at the fact that they would not be in touch for the foreseeable future. Neither she nor her mother had any notion that their loved ones had been deported.

Working at Amsterdam's Centraal station in the weeks and months following the war's end, on 3 June 1945 Jan Gies learned from another survivor that Otto Frank would be returning. That afternoon, almost ten months to the day after he had been arrested, Otto arrived in the city. With nowhere to live, he moved in with Miep and Jan. He knew he had lost his wife, his home and the bulk of his possessions, but still maintained hope that Anne and Margot would also return from the Nazi camps.

The Diary Saved

Every day, Otto checked the Red Cross lists that detailed the thousands of people who were still unaccounted for, the vast majority of them Jews. He also asked other survivors, who were slowly trickling into the city from concentration camps across Europe, for news of his daughters. Anne's sixteenth birthday, 12 June, passed without news. On 18 July, his worst fears were confirmed. Crosses had been placed by both Anne and Margot's names on the survival lists by Janny Brandes-Brilleslijper, who along with her sister Lientje had returned home. He visited Lientje and Janny personally and heard how his daughters had perished in Bergen-Belsen, just a few weeks before the liberation.

Around 107,000 Jews had been deported from the Netherlands between 1942 and 1944, and Otto was one of just 5,200 who returned from the camps alive. Among those also murdered by the Nazis were Anne's school friends Sanne Ledermann and Ilse Wagner. Auguste van Pels, too, did not survive. She was transported from Bergen-Belsen, possibly to Raguhn and then Theresienstadt. Some reports suggest that she was killed after being thrown in front of a train, but her exact fate is unknown. All that is certain is that she did not survive the Nazi camps and died somewhere in Germany or Czechoslovakia shortly before the end of the war, probably in April or May 1945.

Of all the western European countries occupied by the Nazis during World War Two, the Jews of the Netherlands had by far the worst survival record. Some 75 per cent of the pre-war Jewish population was killed in the Final Solution. In France, by contrast, the figures were reversed, with three-quarters of the Jews in the country still alive when the war ended.

When their friends were arrested on 4 August 1944, Miep and Bep had no idea of the tragic fates that would befall them. They had ventured into the Annexe later that day and found Anne's diaries and papers scattered across the floor. They had quickly gathered them together and placed the pile in Miep's desk drawer for safety until Anne came back. Miep also retrieved the shawl Anne wore when combing her hair and some of the Frank family's photo albums, before the Annexe was stripped of furniture and belongings several days later by the Puls removal company, as was common practice after Jews were arrested. Although she and Bep hadn't collected all the papers at first, for fear that the Gestapo would return and find them upstairs, Miep sent Willem van Maaren back into the Annexe with instructions to bring her any more papers he could find, then stowed these with the others in her desk.

The winter of 1944-45 was exceptionally unforgiving to the Dutch. Not only was it bitterly cold, but German blockades resulted in severe food and fuel shortages, resulting in thousands of citizens starving to death. Now known as the *Hongerwinter*, one can only speculate as to how the residents of the Secret Annexe would have fared during this time had they not been betrayed. Hendrik Van Hoeve, the grocer who had supplied Miep with extra produce and carried potatoes to the Prinsengracht, had been arrested in May 1944 for hiding two Jews in his own home and his absence had already impacted on the food supplies in the Annexe prior to the arrest. In February 1945, Miep cycled as far as Kampen, over 80 kilometres from Amsterdam, just to find sustenance for herself and Jan, so whether sufficient food could have been sourced for an additional eight people is questionable.

Miep did not read the diary during the long, harsh winter months, nor did she tell Otto she had saved it when he returned the following summer, hoping as he was that Anne and Margot had also survived, and intending to present it to the writer herself. The day that she learned of Anne's fate, however, her thoughts immediately turned to the drawer of her desk. Anne would not pen any more lines or reclaim her work. Miep gathered the original diary, notebooks and loose papers together and carried them to Otto in his office, placing them in front of him with the words 'here is your daughter Anne's legacy to you'.

Part Four: Posthumous Fame

Publishing Het Achterhuis

Initially, it was too painful for Otto to read Anne's diary, but by late August he wrote to his family that he was managing a few pages a day. As Otto progressed through Anne's writings, he realised he'd never known the deeper side of his youngest daughter's character. The deep-thinking, introspective Anne who shone through in the eloquently written passages was a stranger to the moody, attention-seeking teenager who had so often conflicted with others in the Annexe.

Otto began translating excerpts into German for his family in Switzerland, who could not read Dutch, and also typed sections to circulate among his close friends. Many praised Anne's literary abilities and commended the document as a moving record, both of the war years and of an adolescent's development into adulthood.

As 1945 turned to 1946, Otto decided that Anne's diary should be published. She had, after all, gone a long way towards revising her work with a view to publication and had also written that she wanted to continue living after her death. Thanks to Miep saving Anne's writings, Otto felt he could fulfil his lost daughter's wishes. He worked from both her original diary entries and the revised passages to edit a version of the diary that he felt represented Anne and her ideals, removing unflattering passages about his dead wife and sections about sex and puberty that he believed would be unappealing to publishers.

Otto's initial submissions to Dutch publishing houses were met with rejection, however. Some felt it was too soon after the war to be reminded of painful events, while others did not believe a teenager's diary would be interesting to the reading public. On 3 April 1946, however, an article appeared in a journal called *Het Parool*, written by an academic called Jan Romein who had come across Otto's typed manuscript through an acquaintance. 'A Child's Voice' heralded the diary as a unique document and was instrumental in prompting keen interest from several publishers. Romein wrote that he doubted there were any other wartime diaries 'as lucid, as intelligent, and at the same time as natural' and stated that the manuscript embodied 'all the hideousness of fascism'.

Het Achterhuis, the title Anne herself had chosen, was finally published on 25 June 1947, with the subtitle 'Diary Letters from 14 June 1942 – 1 August 1944'. Otto's original edit had been further abridged to meet the publisher's requirements, but what mattered to him was that his daughter's words were now available in print. The final months of Anne's life, from the arrest in Amsterdam to her death in Bergen-Belsen, were outlined in a brief epilogue comprising just a few sentences. Her personal experiences of Westerbork, deportation, Auschwitz and Bergen-Belsen obviously did not feature in the book, in many ways sparing its readers from the worst horrors of the genocide that would come to be known as the Holocaust.

The initial run of 1,500 copies was well-received in the Netherlands and a second edition appeared before the end of the year. The diary subsequently appeared in

French and German in 1950. In 1952, the same year that Otto moved out of Miep and Jan's home to be with his remaining family in Switzerland, an English edition was published in Britain and the USA under the title *The Diary of a Young Girl*. Although it sold slowly at first in Britain, the *Diary* was an instant success when it hit American bookshops, thanks in part to a rave review by a writer named Meyer Levin in *The New York Times*. The first run of 5,000 copies sold out within a day and a second edition of 15,000 books had to be quickly arranged. Anne Frank was famous.

Broadway and Hollywood

Such was the success of Anne's diary in America that calls swiftly abounded for a stage adaptation of her story. Although reluctant at first, Otto eventually gave his permission, as he envisaged a play as a means for the diary's message to reach a wider audience. He had married Fritzi Markovits-Geiringer in November 1953, an Austrian Jew who had lost her husband and son in the Holocaust but had survived Auschwitz with her daughter Eva, who was the same age as Anne. Fritzi became a great support to Otto as Anne's fame grew.

Meyer Levin, who had promoted *The Diary of a Young Girl* so successfully when it was first published in the USA, was keen to write the script for the play. He did indeed pen an adaptation, however it was not deemed suitable and the job eventually went to the husband and wife team of Albert Hackett and Frances Goodrich Hackett. Levin, bitterly disappointed, continued to hound Otto about the rights to the stage adaptation for years, leading to several stressful lawsuits. Nevertheless, *The Diary of Anne Frank* as penned by the Hacketts opened on Broadway on 5 October 1955, starring a young actress called Susan Strasberg as Anne. It was a great success with the American public and won the Pulitzer Prize for drama and the Tony Award for Best Play.

The Hacketts' play ends with one of the most quoted lines from Anne's diary, that despite everything taking place in the world around her, she still believes people are good at heart. This positive sentiment was taken out of context, from a passage in which Anne describes the difficulty of maintaining youthful optimism in a time of war and discrimination. Whether Anne maintained this belief in humanity through her suffering in Auschwitz and Bergen-Belsen is questionable, but her words are nonetheless employed on the stage to demonstrate the triumph of the human spirit when living in fear.

In November 1956 the play premiered in Amsterdam, with the Dutch Queen Juliana in the audience. Otto never went to see *The Diary of Anne Frank*. He felt it would be too painful to watch the past acted out on stage and respectfully declined all invitations. Miep, Kugler and the other helpers did see it, however, as did Anne's cousin Buddy Elias, himself an actor. With the exception of the Frank family, Anne's pseudonyms were used for all the characters in the play, though Peter retained his real first name. When it was first performed in Germany, also in 1956, it was instrumental in breaking barriers and prompting discussion about the persecution of Jews during the war. Sales of the diary subsequently rocketed in the country of Anne's birth and in 1958 the play was Germany's most performed piece of theatre.

The stage adaptation of Anne's diary was revived in 1997 and continues to draw audiences around the world. Interestingly, except for the scholarly *Critical Edition*, the diary itself has never been published in English under the title *The Diary of Anne Frank*, though many people refer to it as such – testament, perhaps, to the enduring legacy of the play, or more likely a sign that the title *The Diary of a Young Girl* has never ingrained itself in the public consciousness as much as the name of its author, whose image graces every cover.

Given the play's success on Broadway, it was perhaps inevitable that Hollywood would follow suit. *The Diary of Anne Frank*, based on the play and directed by George Stevens, opened in cinemas in March 1959. Shot in black and white, the film ran to almost three hours and won three Academy Awards, including Best Supporting Actress for Shelley Winters as Mrs van Daan.

Both the film and the stage production took some liberties with the characterisation of certain people integral to the story, notably Fritz Pfeffer, who as Albert Dussel provided a comedic presence in both pieces. On first reading the script, Otto had objected to the portrayal of Pfeffer, however his concerns were largely ignored. Lotte Kaletta, who had married Pfeffer posthumously and been on excellent terms with Otto since the war, was outraged by the adaptation's presentation of her beloved Fritz, particularly the manner in which he was shown as being ignorant of Jewish traditions. He had, in fact, been the most religious of all the hidden Jews, leading the weekly Sabbath prayers in the Annexe. Lotte subsequently severed her ties with Otto and refused to grant interviews about her partner.

Hendrik van Hoeve, the grocer, had survived the war and appeared in the film as himself. Some of the original Broadway cast reprised their roles for the movie but a new actress had to be found to play Anne. Otto was keen for Audrey Hepburn to have the part, but she politely refused, appreciating that she was too old to play a teenager, though Anne's story had a particular resonance for her since she had grown up in the Netherlands during the war. The role instead went to one Millie Perkins, a model. Many actresses have portrayed the young diarist in subsequent film and television adaptations, with each incarnation either influencing the general public's perception of Anne Frank or conflicting with their ideal of her.

Both the 1955 play and the 1959 film contributed to the ideal of Anne as a symbol of belief in the innate goodness of humanity. Although they arguably Americanized and universalized Anne's story, to an extent diminishing the Jewish aspect of its historical context, both the play and the film helped to fulfil Otto's hope that the diary's message of tolerance and optimism would reach as many people as possible. Even in the twenty-first century, however, members of the stage and screen audiences occasionally remain unaware that the dramatizations they have watched are based on real people and events.

The Anne Frank House

Otto resumed his position as head of Opekta in 1945. After *Het Achterhuis* was published two years later, members of the public began appearing at the Prinsengracht offices, asking to look round the rooms where Anne had hidden during the Occupation. Kleiman and Kugler, who had both returned safely from work camps after being arrested in 1944, gave informal tours to such visitors.

263 Prinsengracht was a 17th century structure and in the early 1950s, Opekta was informed that new company premises would have to be found, as a developer wanted to tear down the already-weak building. There was public outcry over the proposed demolition and Kleiman, along with others, established the Anne Frank Stichting in an endeavour to preserve the offices and the Annexe. Enough funds were raised to save the building and on 3 May 1960, it was officially opened as a museum. Johannes Kleiman sadly did not live to see the opening, as he died in his office in 1959, at the age of sixty-three. Nevertheless, along with the other helpers, in 1972 he was honoured by Yad Vashem, Israel's official memorial to the Holocaust, as being 'Righteous Among the Nations' for his part in assisting the Franks, van Pelses and Pfeffer during the war.

Otto wished for an education centre to be incorporated into 263 Prinsengracht, teaching visitors about the importance of equality and tolerance. He also stipulated that the Annexe remain unfurnished, left in the same state as when it was emptied in August 1944. Aside from a period of renovation in 1970-71, The Anne Frank House, as it is called, has remained open to the public ever since, even during further major renovations and restoration work in the 1990s.

Anne's picture postcards, the map charting the Allied invasion and the pencil marks showing how the Frank sisters grew during their voluntary imprisonment still remain on the Annexe walls. Although it is no longer safe to enter the attic above Peter's room, a mirror permits visitors to see the view from the small window. The chestnut tree that Anne so admired can no longer be seen, however, as it fell down following a storm in August 2010. Saplings from the original tree were being grown from 2005 and have been planted around the world as memorials to Anne and the other victims of genocide, in addition to being symbols of new life.

The offices where the Opekta staff carried out their daily business were refurnished to resemble their wartime appearance during the renovations in the 1990s with assistance from Miep Gies, who outlived all the other helpers and died at the age of 100 in January 2010. Anne's original chequered diary is on display in the museum, on permanent loan from the Netherlands Institute for War Documentation, and the Oscar won by Shelley Winters for her portrayal of Mrs Van Daan is exhibited outside the café. In the 21st century, Anne's story has also been made into a graphic novel and the Anne Frank House launched a smartphone app in early 2012 to allow tourists to envisage Amsterdam as it would have been during Anne's youth. A partner organisation in Berlin, the Anne Frank Zentrum, also tells the story of the Frank family and those who shared their hiding place, with a facsimile copy of the original diary and a photographic exhibition.

The Anne Frank House has become one of Amsterdam's most popular tourist attractions and is among the most visited museums in Europe, with over one million people passing through its doors every year since 2007.

Authenticating the Diary

In the 1950s, 60s and 70s, several allegations denouncing the diary's authenticity were circulated. As Anne Frank became a household name, Otto had to contend with these neo-Nazi assertions that her diary was a fake. The first known attacks were published in a Swedish newspaper in late 1957, claiming that the diary was mainly written by Meyer Levin. In 1958, Lothar Stielau asserted that the published versions of Anne's diary did not match any original text she may have written. The Meyer Levin idea was promulgated again in the summer of 1967, while in 1978 Ditlieb Felderer, a prominent Holocaust denier, published the defamatory *Anne Frank – A Hoax?*

Such attacks often led to drawn-out, emotionally straining court cases for Otto, who naturally found it extremely upsetting that people should denigrate the work of his dead daughter. Miep, Jan and Bep all testified in a German court that they had known Anne was keeping a diary between 1942 and 1944, and experts were called upon to examine the original handwriting as early as 1959, yet the critics persisted. Indeed, although Holocaust denial is illegal in many countries, it exists to this day and Anne's diary continues to occasionally be a target for neo-Nazis and anti-Semites.

Even in his later years, Otto continued to fight claims of inauthenticity on behalf of his youngest daughter, yet he always advocated tolerance and was known for his humanistic outlook on life. He devoted his time to spreading Anne's message around the world and Fritzi assisted him closely with answering the enormous correspondence he received pertaining to the diary. Although Anne, in many ways, became a driving force for Otto, on the rare occasions he mentioned his eldest daughter his most frequent words were that Margot had been an angel.

In 1963, with Fritzi, Otto established the Anne Frank-Fonds in Basle, which is responsible for the copyrights of Anne's work and manages all royalties deriving from sales of the diary. His nephew, Leni's son Buddy Elias, was president of the Fonds from 1996 until his death in March 2015. It is an entirely separate organisation to Anne Frank Stichting in Amsterdam, which continues to maintain the premises at 263 Prinsengracht.

Otto died of lung cancer on 19 August 1980, at the age of 91. After his death, the Netherlands Institute for War Documentation, to which he had willed Anne's material writings, conducted an official investigation into all her work in an effort to combat ongoing claims of inauthenticity. Meticulous research proved the materials were all in use before 1944 and a detailed analysis of Anne's handwriting demonstrated that, beyond the shadow of a doubt, this was all the work of one person, carried out over a two-year period. The diary's authenticity had been scientifically, conclusively proven.

These findings were published in the Dutch *Critical Edition* of 1986, with an English translation appearing in 1989. This hefty academic tome, besides giving readers a detailed overview of the investigations alongside articles about the historical context and the Frank family, presents all three versions of the diary side by side. Version A constitutes Anne's original entries from 12 June 1942 to 1 August 1944, although her original notebook for almost all of 1943 has never been found. Version B is the revised entries she wrote with a view to publishing *Het Achterhuis* and includes her reworked passages for 1943. Version C is the text Otto edited that was published as *The Diary of a Young Girl*, with excerpts taken from both Anne's A and B versions, as well as material from her sketches about life in the Secret Annexe. The magnitude of Anne's own rewriting is immediately evident to any reader of the Critical Edition, and the literary feat is even more astonishing when one remembers that she had barely turned fifteen when she was forced to stop.

Although Otto left his daughter's writings to the Netherlands Institute for War Documentation in his will, in 1998 five pages emerged that previously had been kept secret. Otto had given them to his friend Cor Suijk for safekeeping, apparently not wanting them published in his lifetime as they contained speculations about whether his marriage to Edith was entirely happy. When their survival became known, it sparked something of a media frenzy and again prompted conjecture about whether the diary was genuine. These pages have since been officially authenticated and published in *The Diary of a Young Girl*: *The Definitive Edition*, and in the *Revised Critical Edition*. The copyright, like that of all Anne's writing, remains with the Anne Frank-Fonds.

Who Betrayed Anne Frank?

An investigation in to who betrayed the eight Jews hiding at 263 Prinsengracht took place in 1948. No conclusions were reached. As Anne's diary became globally renowned, the betrayer's identity became something of a public cause, with indignation abounding that nobody had been brought to justice for tipping off the Gestapo.

In her diary, Anne wrote how the Annexe residents were wary of Willem van Maaren, who replaced Bep's father, Mr Voskuijl, as warehouse manager when he became ill in 1943. Van Maaren was intensely curious about the rooms at the back of the building and noticed that unusually large amounts of food were delivered to the offices. He purposefully left traps downstairs, supposedly to catch thieves, and asked the Opekta staff uncomfortable questions about the Annexe. When questioned about the betrayal in 1948 and 1964, van Maaren admitted his suspicions but repeatedly denied informing the Gestapo. He died in 1971.

Karl Josef Silberbauer, the arresting officer, was tracked down in the early 1960s, but did not know who made the fateful phone call betraying the Franks, the van Pelses and Pfeffer. He had been acting on the orders of superiors and said he had not received the tip-off personally. Otto, advocating tolerance over vengeance after his experiences, chose not to pursue the enquiries and the case was once again closed. However, two more recent theories diverted attention from the often-accused van Maaren and prompted the Netherlands Institute for War Documentation to re-open the case in 2003.

In her 1998 biography of Anne, Melissa Müller pointed a finger at Lena van Bladeren-Hartog, a cleaner at 263 Prinsengracht whose husband worked in the warehouse. Lena gossiped with another woman that there were Jews hiding in the building. The rumour that it was a woman who made the call to the Gestapo remains unfounded, however, and Lena died in June 1963. Another person suspected of being the informant was Tonny Ahlers who was, according to Otto Frank's biographer Carol Ann Lee, a vicious anti-Semite who blackmailed Otto both during and after the war. Records testify that Ahlers betrayed several Jews during the Occupation and was arrested for other crimes. According to Ahlers' brother and children, he admitted betraying the Franks, however no official records verify this and Ahlers died in 2000.

The 2003 investigation concluded that, while the case against Ahlers was strong, all evidence was circumstantial. Along with Hartog and van Maaren, his name was cleared. In 2015, a new suspect was named: a sister of Bep Voskuijl. Nelly Voskuijl, aged 21 in 1944, was apparently a Nazi collaborator who may have guessed that her sister and father were helping to shelter Jews at their workplace. Once again, however, there is no hard evidence to support this theory and Nelly's death in 2001 renders this line of enquiry near impossible to pursue.

It is entirely possible that the Franks, van Pelses and Pfeffer went some way towards betraying themselves through carelessness during their twenty-five months in the Annexe. After the war, people from the surrounding buildings reported that they had thought something unusual was going on at 263 Prinsengracht: the twitch of a curtain, an open window, coughing in the night and a toilet flushing were all signs of residence in a building that should have been empty. For so many people to have remained hidden for so long without detection would have been no mean feat and it is perhaps unsurprising that suspicions were aroused. What prompted someone to act on these suspicions, however, remains unknown.

Betrayals were reasonably common during the Occupation. Of approximately 25,000 Jews who went into hiding in the Netherlands, some 9,000 eventually found themselves in the hands of the authorities. Informants received financial compensation and war-induced poverty or fear of the Nazis may have been instrumental in many Dutch citizens' decisions to turn in Jews and resistance workers. Whether money, fear, or anti-Semitism was the motive for whoever betrayed Anne and the seven other Jews hiding at 263 Prinsengracht will probably never be known and the identity of the caller will likewise remain forever anonymous. All that is certain is somebody telephoned the Gestapo on 4 August 1944, knowing that, in all probability, innocent people would consequently be sent to their deaths.

Anne's Legacy

Anne Frank has been called the most famous girl of the 20th century, the symbol of the Holocaust and an emblem of faith in humanity. *Het Achterhuis* has been translated into nearly seventy languages and has sold over thirty million copies. Thanks to Miep saving her papers and Otto's efforts to publish her work, Anne's wishes of becoming a famous writer and living on after her death have been fulfilled.

Whether it is right that one teenager has come to symbolize the suffering of some six million who died in the Holocaust is debateable, but Anne's face is recognized globally as the most well-known victim of the Nazi genocide. Besides a wide readership in the Western world, the *Diary* is also particularly popular in Japan, where Anne Frank roses are grown and a girl's first menstruation is known as having one's 'Anne Frank day'. The Montessori School in Amsterdam is now called the Anne Frank School and there are streets named after the young writer in Europe, Israel and beyond.

While Broadway and Hollywood were instrumental in making Anne Frank a household name in the mid-20th century, the *Diary* itself remains a set text in many schools. Otto's vision that his daughter's writing should be employed to teach people about the importance of tolerance, equality and hope has also extended to Anne Frank exhibitions that travel around the world and various charitable organisations, including the Anne Frank Trust in the UK. The apartment at 37 Merwedeplein, where the Frank family lived for nearly nine years, is not open to the public but instead provides a haven for writers from around the world who face discrimination in their home countries.

Anne has acquired an almost saintly posthumous reputation in some spheres, which is at odds with the girl who commented on her personal faults with such astute self-recognition. She was overbearing, vain and demanding, but also intelligent, humorous and optimistic. The fanatical racism of the Nazi regime forced her into hiding, accelerating her development into an introspective young woman with a considerable talent for writing. When she died, she left the world an unparalleled account, not only of life as a Jew in hiding during World War Two, but of a teenage girl's personal development and determination to stay positive about life in the face of extreme adversity.

Anne Frank's story is just one among millions of individuals who also lost their lives or suffered during the Holocaust; a generation of voices that were extinguished. Had she not had such an undeniable flair for expressing herself in writing, and had the scattered papers on which she wrote had not been rescued from an attic floor seven decades ago, it is a story the world may never have known.

Select Bibliography

Anne Frank Stichting, *Anne Frank House: A Museum with a Story* (Amsterdam: Anne Frank Stichting, 2001)

Anne Frank Stichting, *Anne Frank in the Secret Annexe: Who Was Who?* (Amsterdam: Anne Frank Stichting, ePub edition, 2013)

Barnouw, David and Stroom, Gerald van der (eds.), *The Diary of Anne Frank: The Revised Critical Edition* (New York: Doubleday, 2003)

Colley, Rupert, *Nazi Germany: History in an Hour* (London: HarperPress, ePub edition, 2011)

Coster, Theo, *We All Wore Stars: Memories of Anne Frank from Her Classmates* (New York: Palgrave Macmillan, 2011)

Frank, Otto and Pressler, Mirjam (eds.), *The Diary of A Young Girl: The Definitive Edition* (London: Puffin Books, 2002)

Gies, Miep with Gold, Alison Leslie, *Anne Frank Remembered: The Story of the Woman Who Helped to Hide the Frank Family* (New York: Simon & Schuster, 1988)

Gold, Alison Leslie, *Hannah Goslar Remembers: A Childhood Friend of Anne Frank* (London: Bloomsbury, 1998)

Kirschenblatt-Gimblett and Shandler, Jeffrey (eds.), *Anne Frank Unbound: Media. Imagination. Memory* (Indiana: Indiana University Press, 2012)

Last, Dick van Galen and Wolfswinkel, Rolf, *Anne Frank and After: Dutch Holocaust Literature in Historical Perspective* (Amsterdam: Amsterdam University Press, 1996)

Lee, Carol Ann, *Roses From The Earth: The Biography of Anne Frank* (London: Viking, 1999)

Lee, Carol Ann, *The Hidden Life of Otto Frank* (London: Penguin Books, 2003)

Lindwer, Willy, *The Last Seven Months of Anne Frank* (London: Young Picador, 2004)

Maarsen, Jacqueline van, *My Name Is Anne, She Said, Anne Frank* (London: Arcadia Books, 2008)

Maarsen, Jacqueline van, *Inheriting Anne Frank* (London: Arcadia Books, 2009)

Müller, Melissa, *Anne Frank: The Biography* (London: Bloomsbury, 2000)

Neville, Peter, *The Holocaust* (Cambridge: Cambridge University Press, 1999)

Pressler, Mirjam, *The Story of Anne Frank* (London: Macmillan, 1999)

Pressler, Mirjam with Elias, Gerti, *Treasures from the Attic: The Extraordinary Story of Anne Frank's Family* (London: Phoenix, 2012)

Prose, Francine, *Anne Frank: The Book, The Life, The Afterlife* (New York: HarperCollins, 2009)

Rees, Lawrence, *Auschwitz, The Nazis and the Final Solution* (London: BBC Books, 2005)

Saunders, Jemma J., *The Holocaust: History in an Hour* (London: William Collins, ePub edition, 2013)

Schloss, Eva with Bartlett, Karen, *After Auschwitz: A Story of Heartbreak and Survival by the Stepsister of Anne Frank* (London: Hodder & Stoughton, 2013)

Schnabel, Ernst, *The Footsteps of Anne Frank* (Harpenden: Southbank Publishing, 2014)

Printed in Great Britain
by Amazon